This Book Belongs to:

_____

"By faith Noah, being warned of God of things not seen as yet, moved with fear, prepared an ark to the saving of his house; by the which he condemned the world, and became heir of the righteousness which is by faith."

Hebrews 11:17

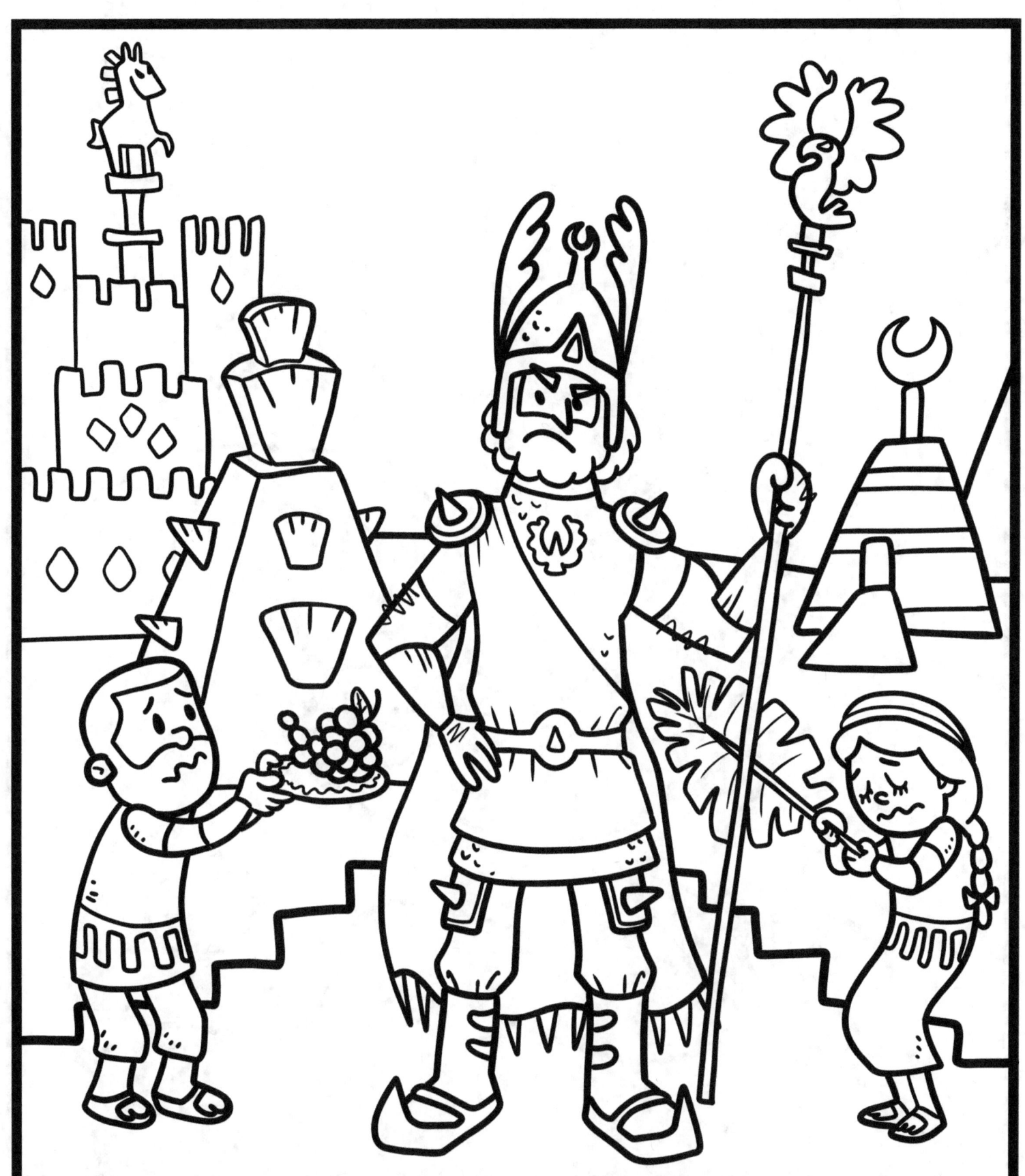

There were giants in the earth in those days; and also after that, when the sons of God came in unto the daughters of men, and they bare children to them, the same became mighty men which were of old, men of renown.

Genesis 6:4

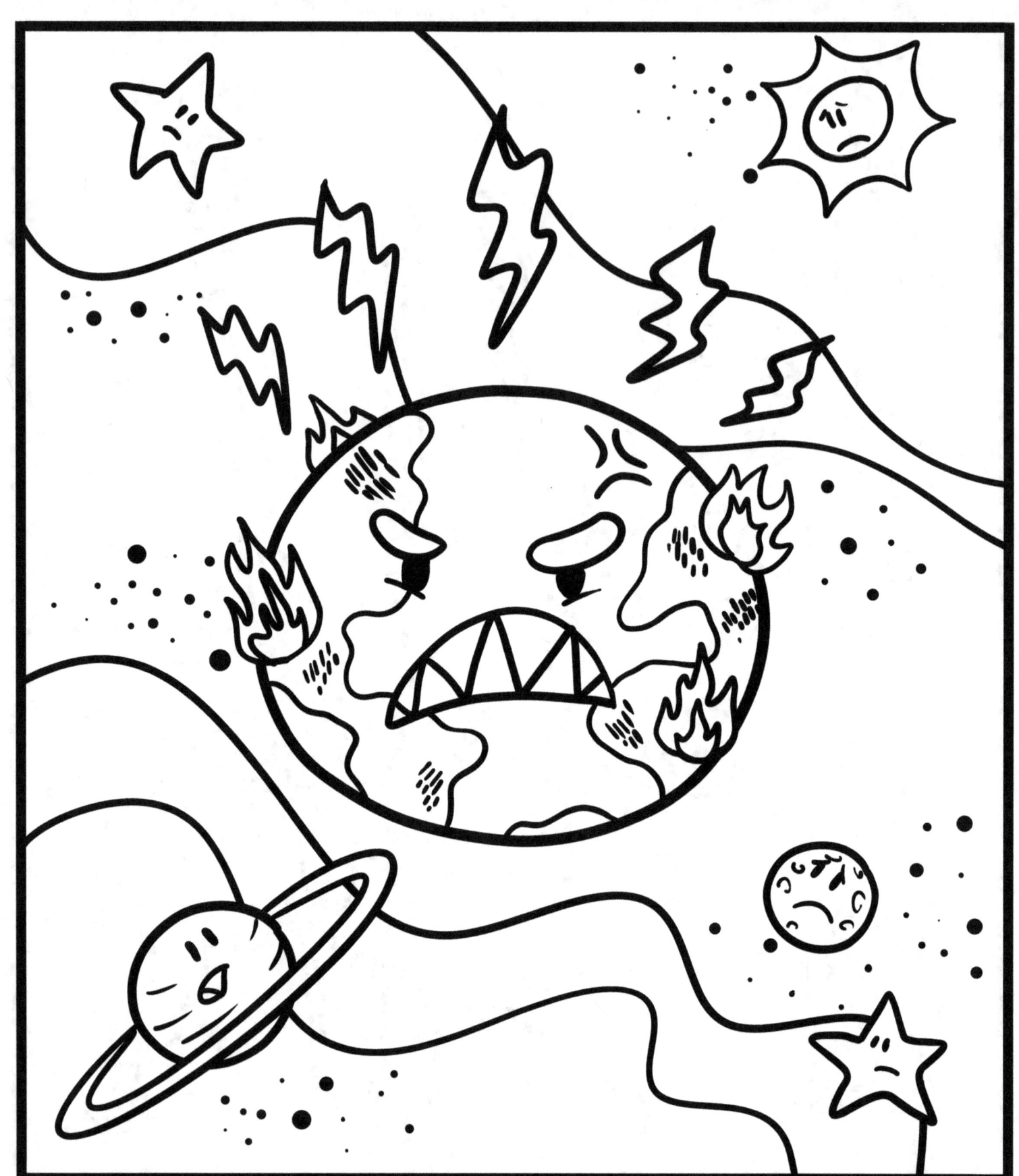

And God saw that the wickedness of man was great in the earth, and that every imagination of the thoughts of his heart was only evil continually.

Genesis 6:5

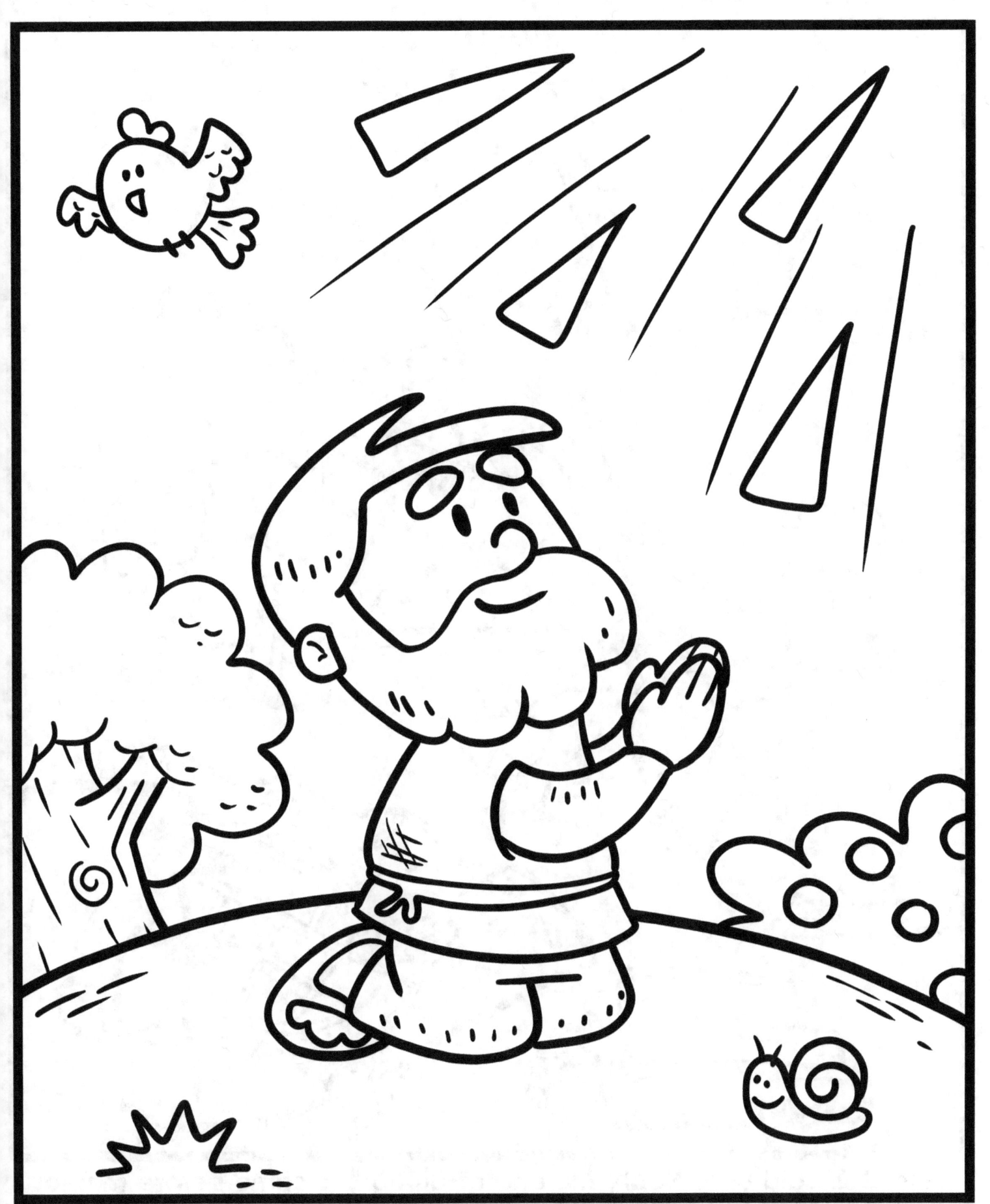

But Noah found grace in the eyes of the Lord.
Genesis 6:8

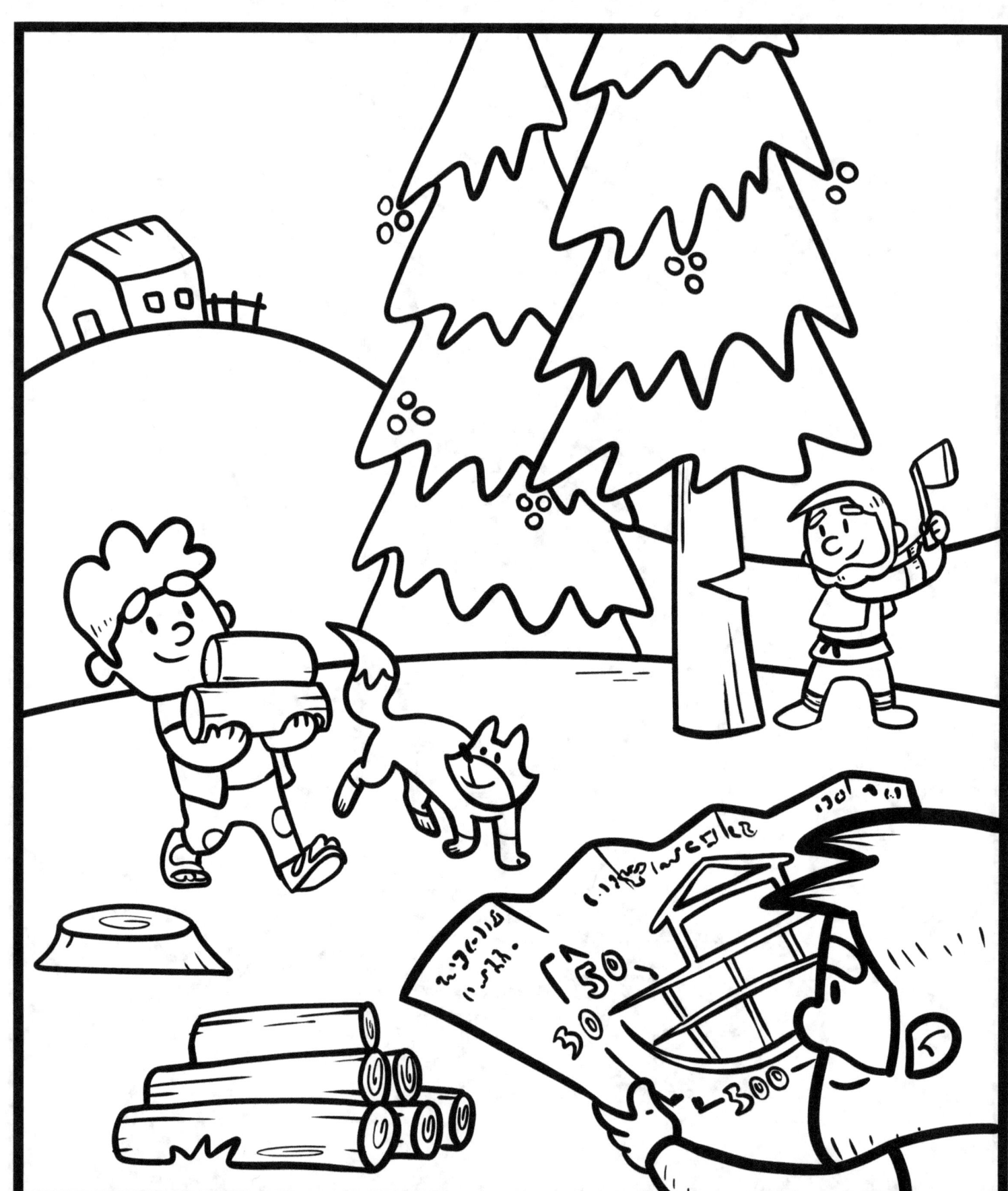

And God said unto Noah, The end of all flesh is come before me; for the earth is filled with violence through them; and, behold, I will destroy them with the earth. Make thee an ark of gopher wood; rooms shalt thou make in the ark...

Genesis 6:13-14a

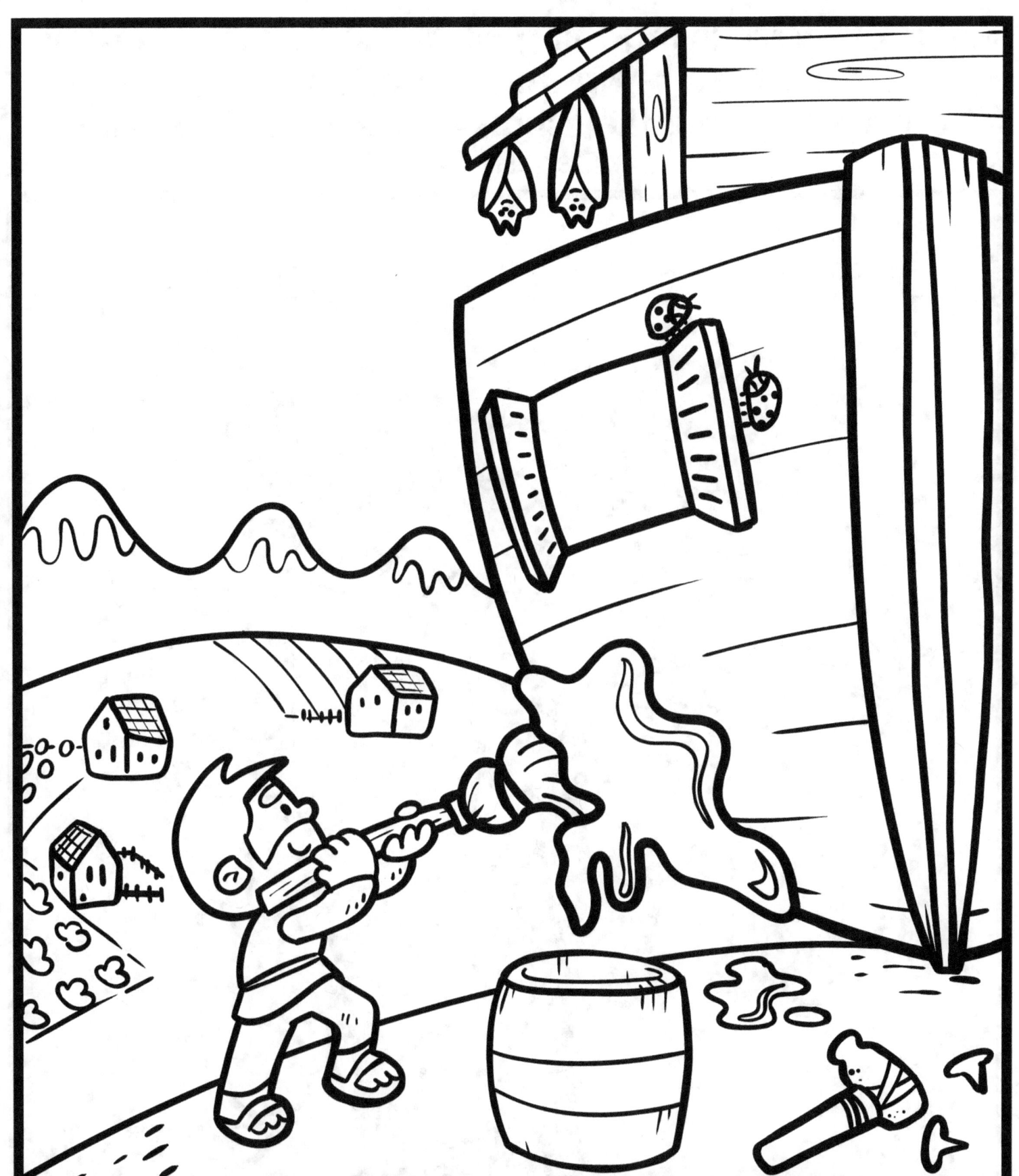

...and shalt pitch it within and without with pitch. And this is the fashion which thou shalt make it of: The length of the ark shall be three hundred cubits, the breadth of it fifty cubits, and the height of it thirty cubits. A window shalt thou make to the ark, and in a cubit shalt thou finish it above; and the door of the ark shalt thou set in the side thereof; with lower, second, and third stories shalt thou make it.

Genesis 6:14b-16

And of every living thing of all flesh, two of every sort shalt thou bring into the ark, to keep them alive with thee; they shall be male and female.
Genesis 6:19

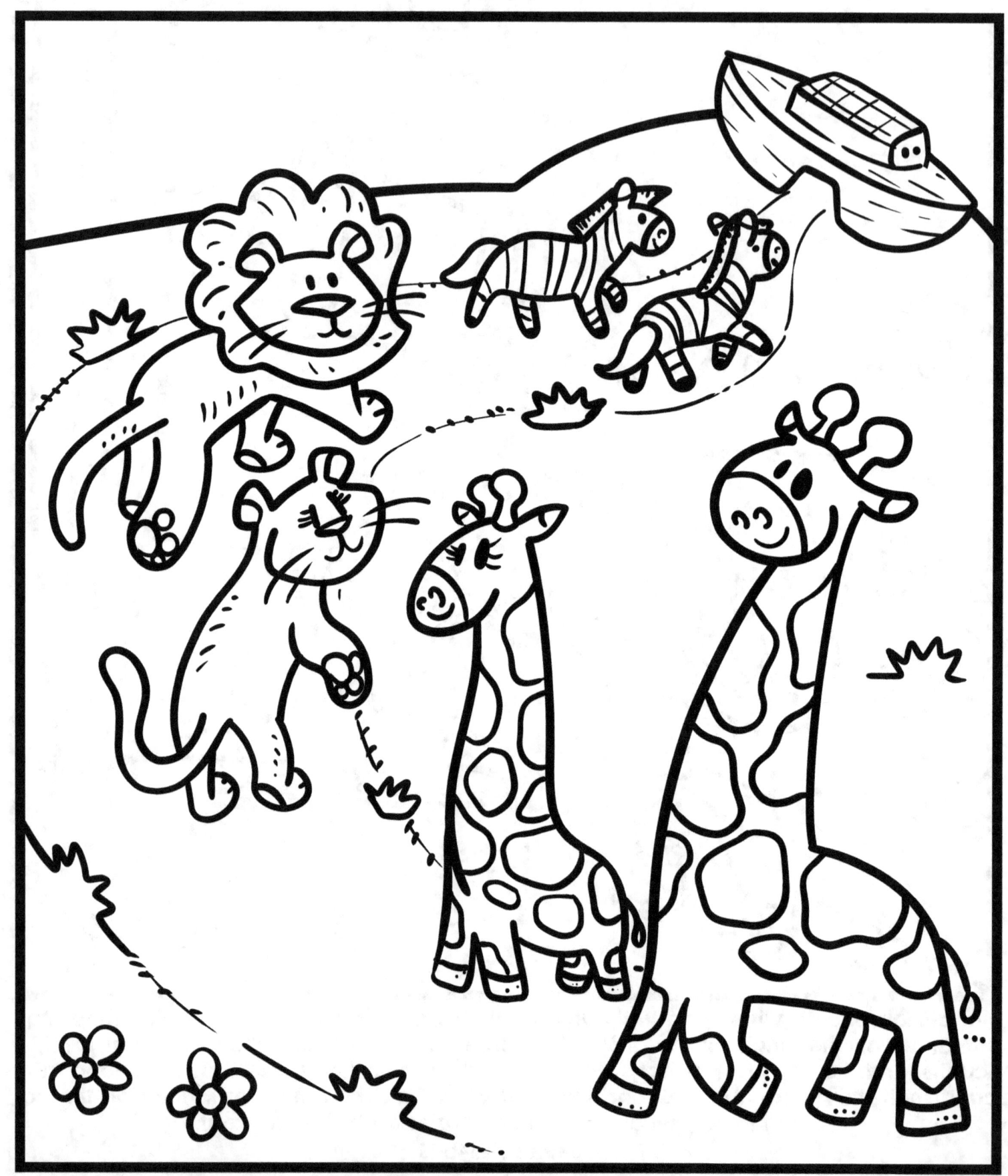

Of fowls after their kind...
Genesis 6:20

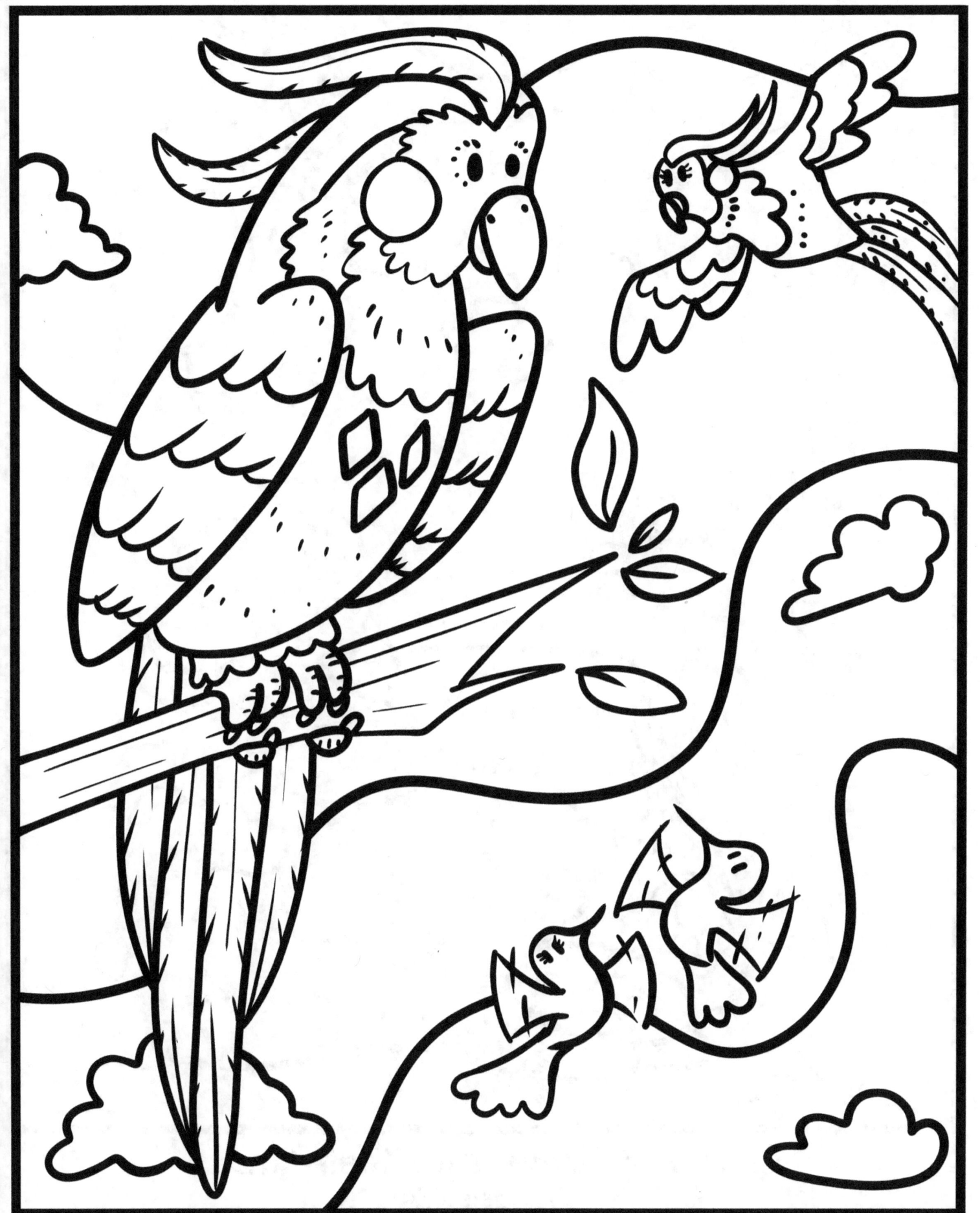

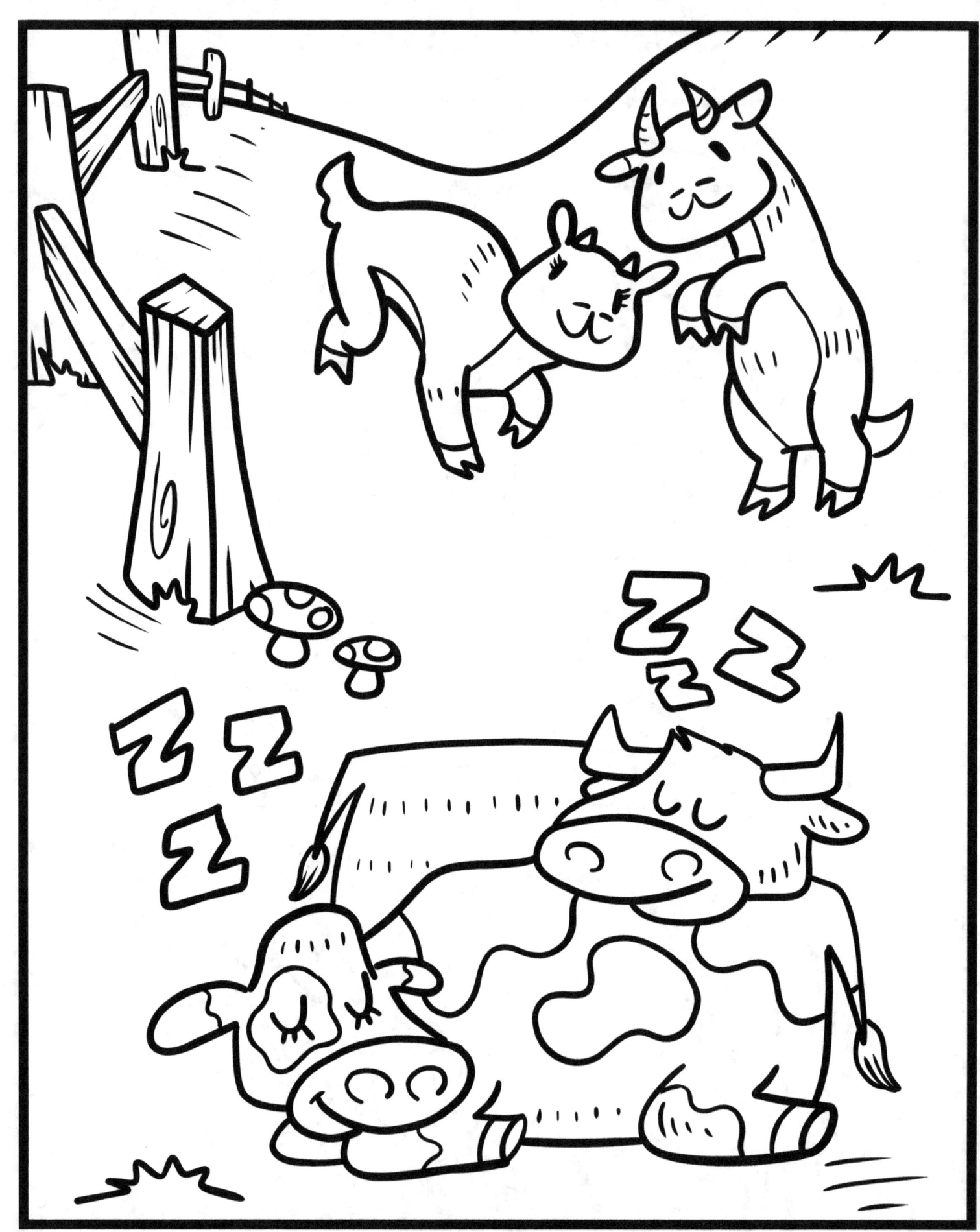

...and of cattle after their kind...
Genesis 6:20

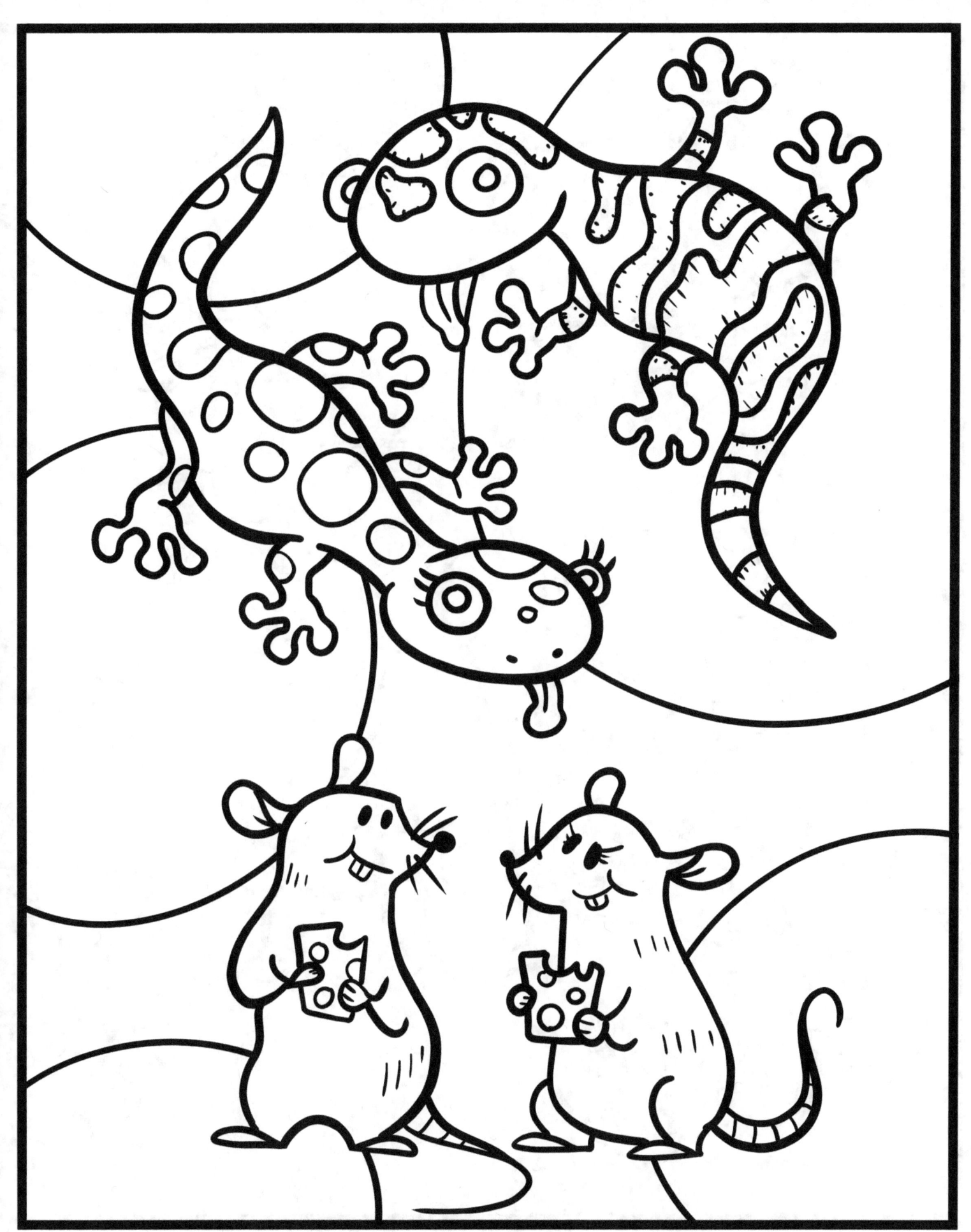

...of every creeping thing of the earth after his kind...
Genesis 6:20

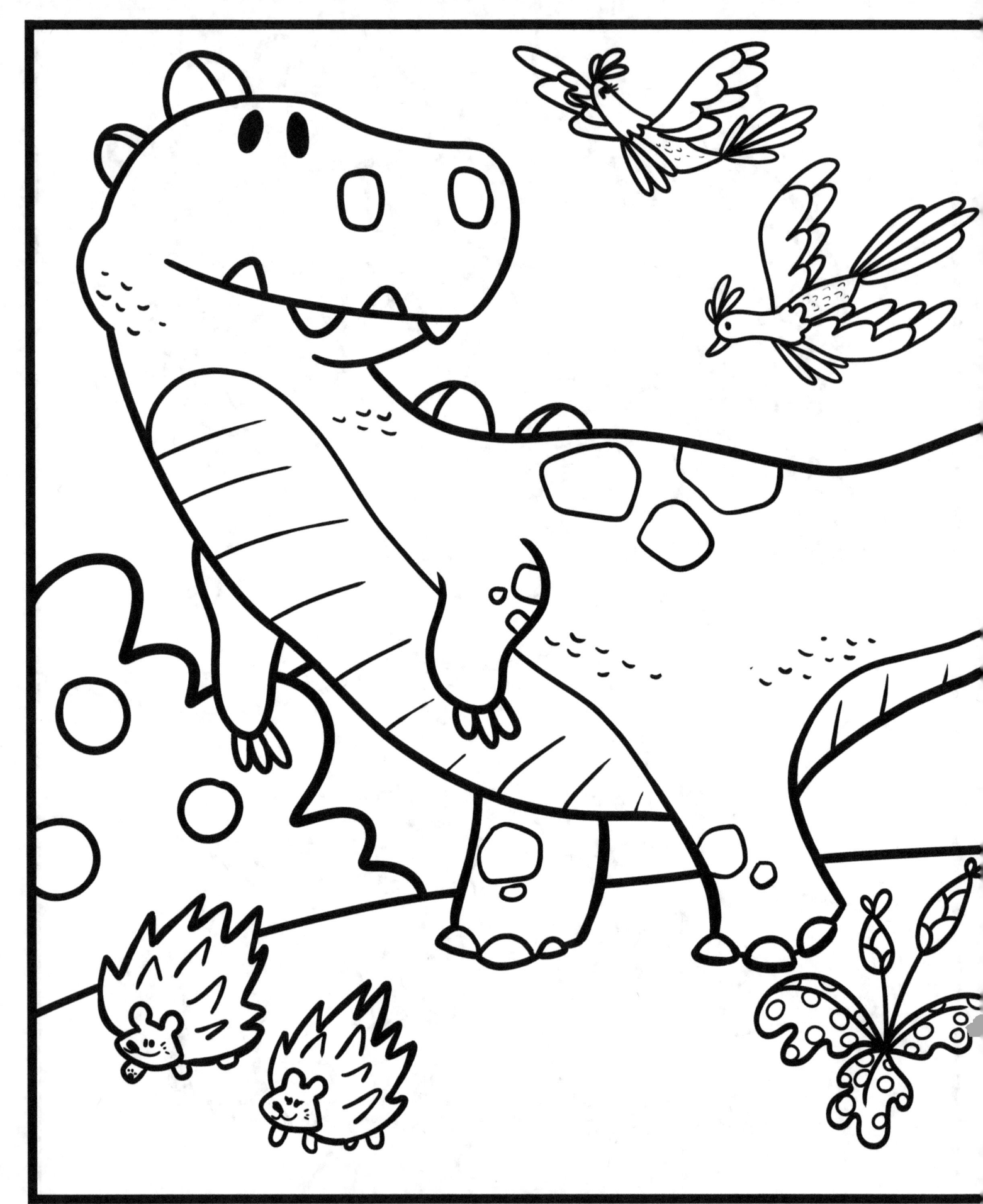

...two of every sort shall come unto thee.
Genesis 6:20

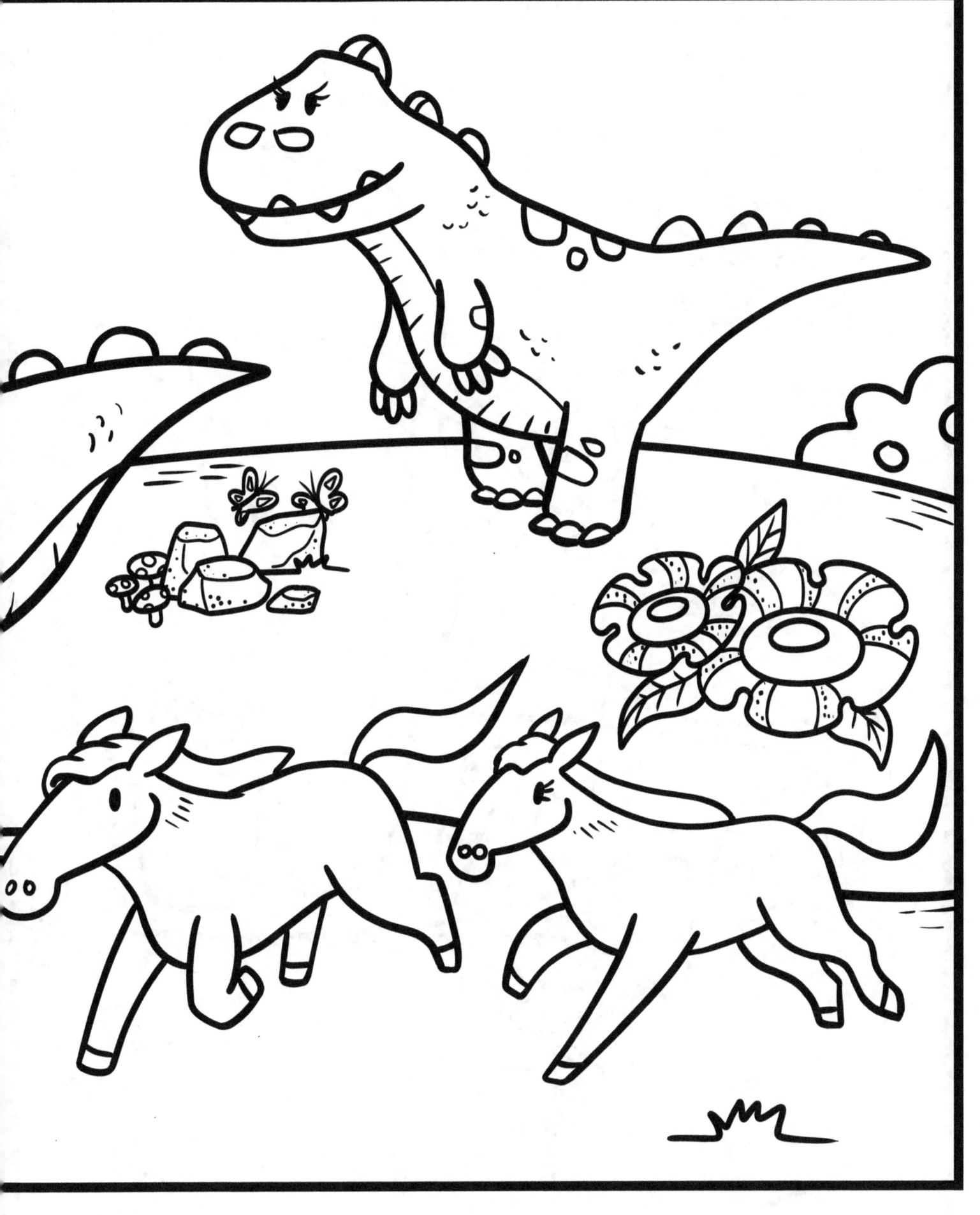

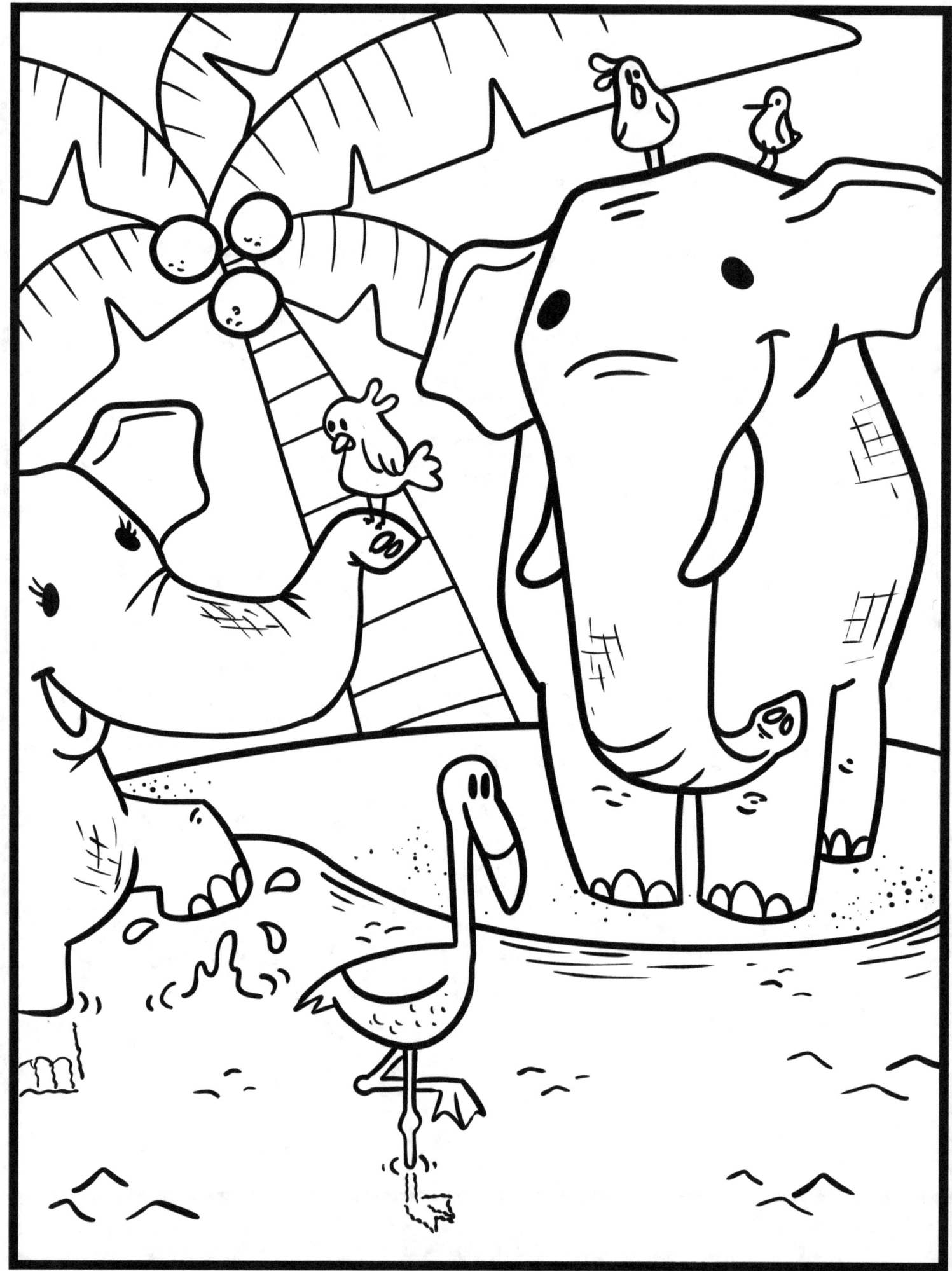

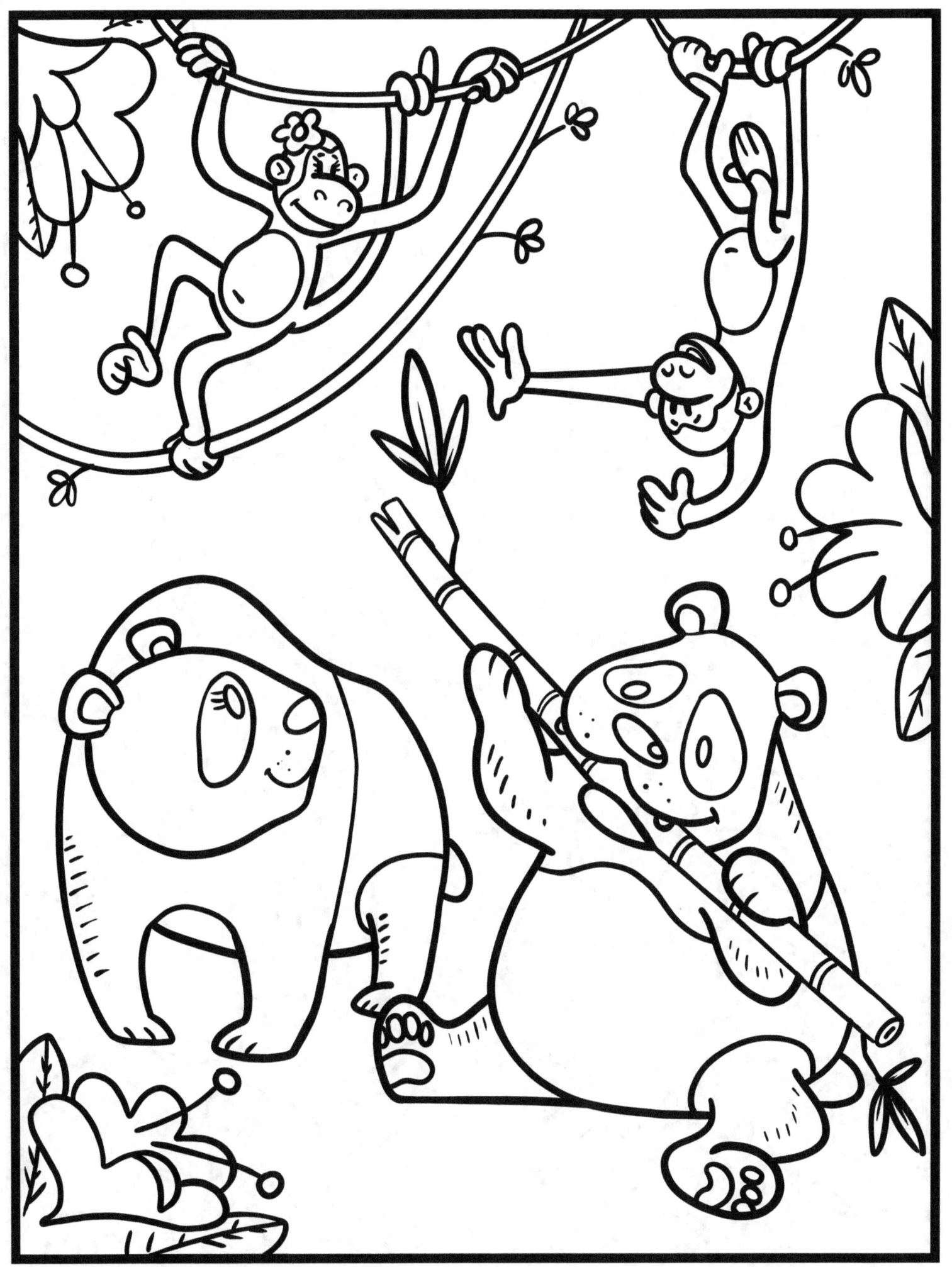

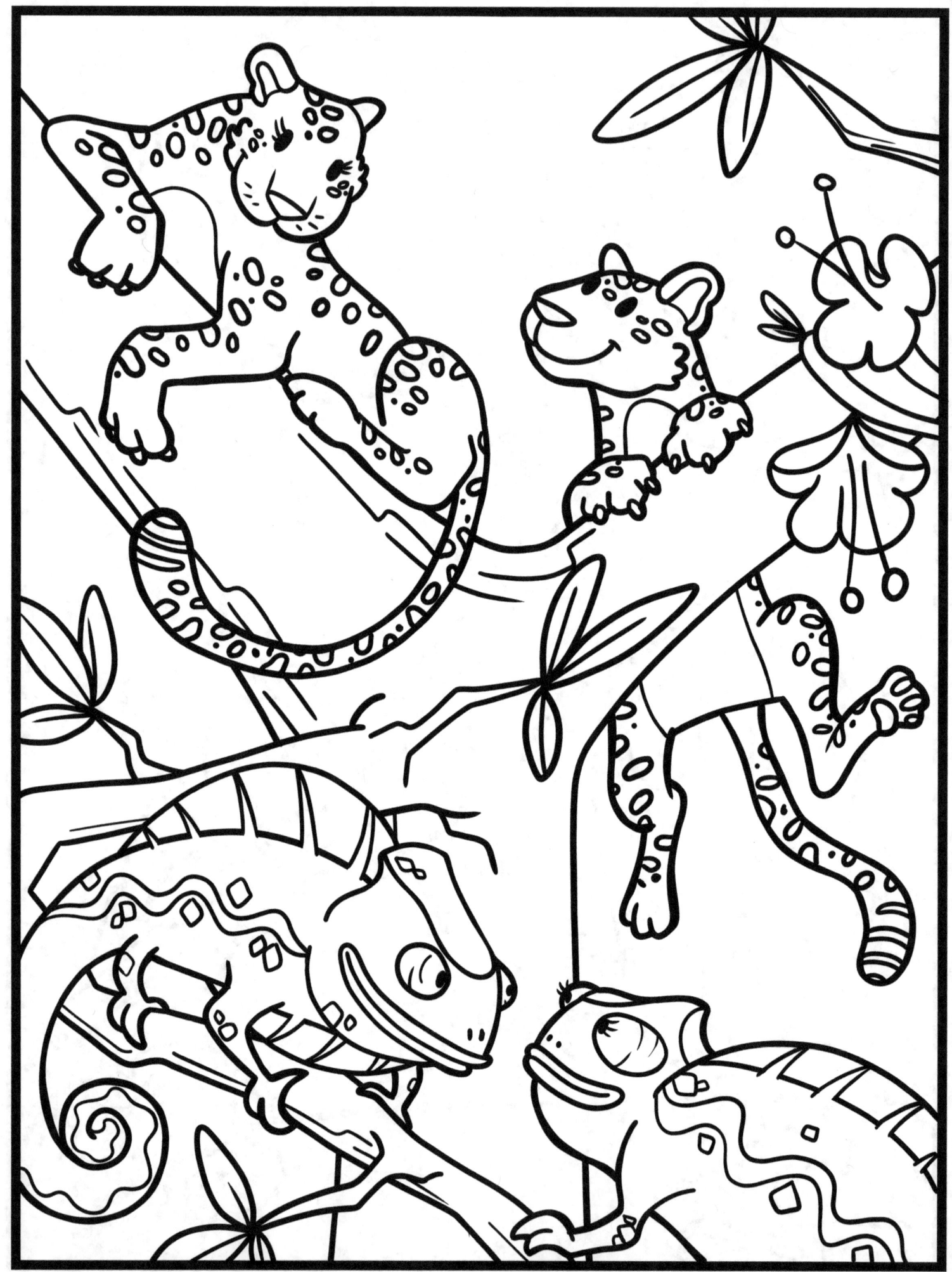

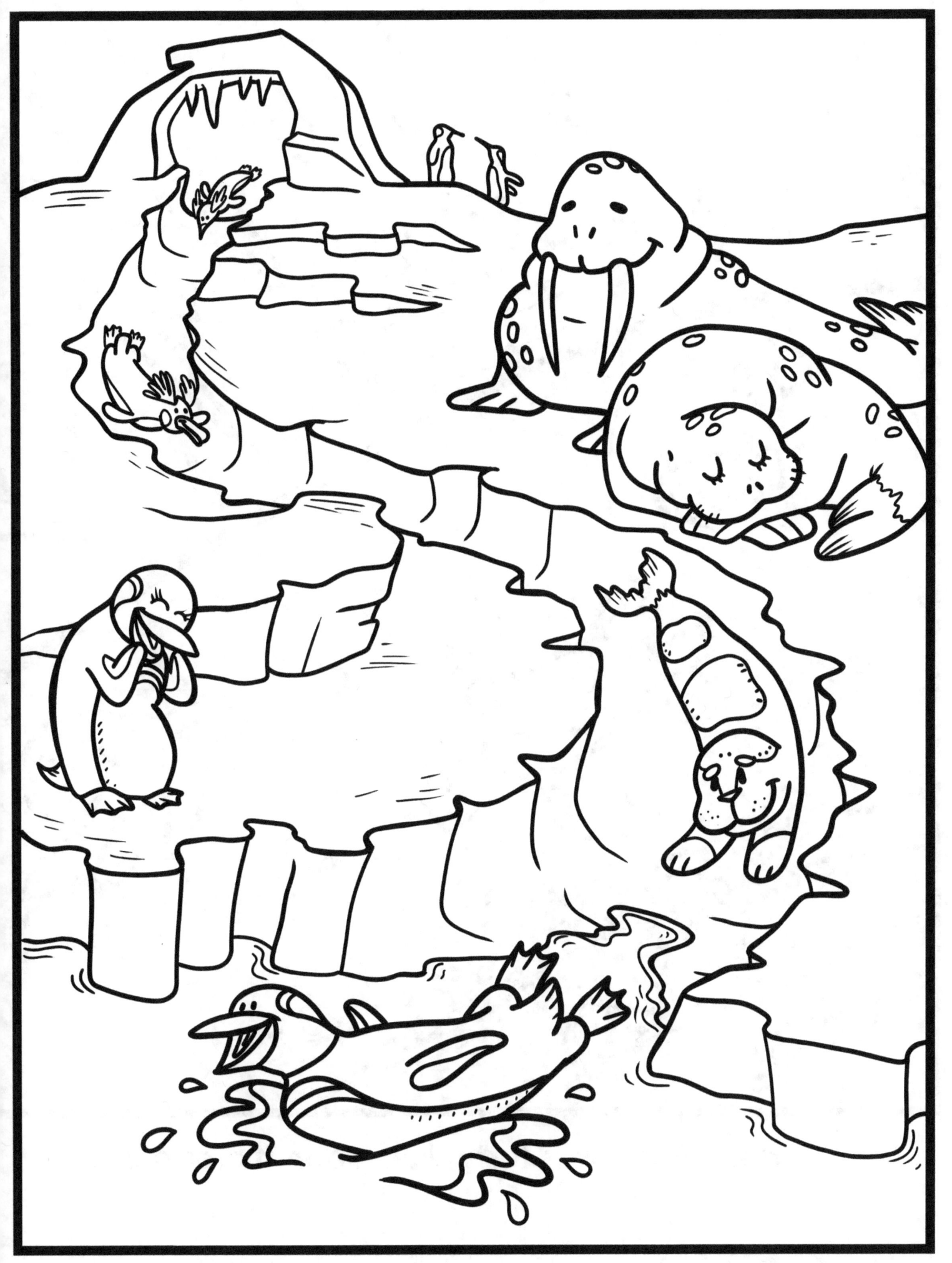

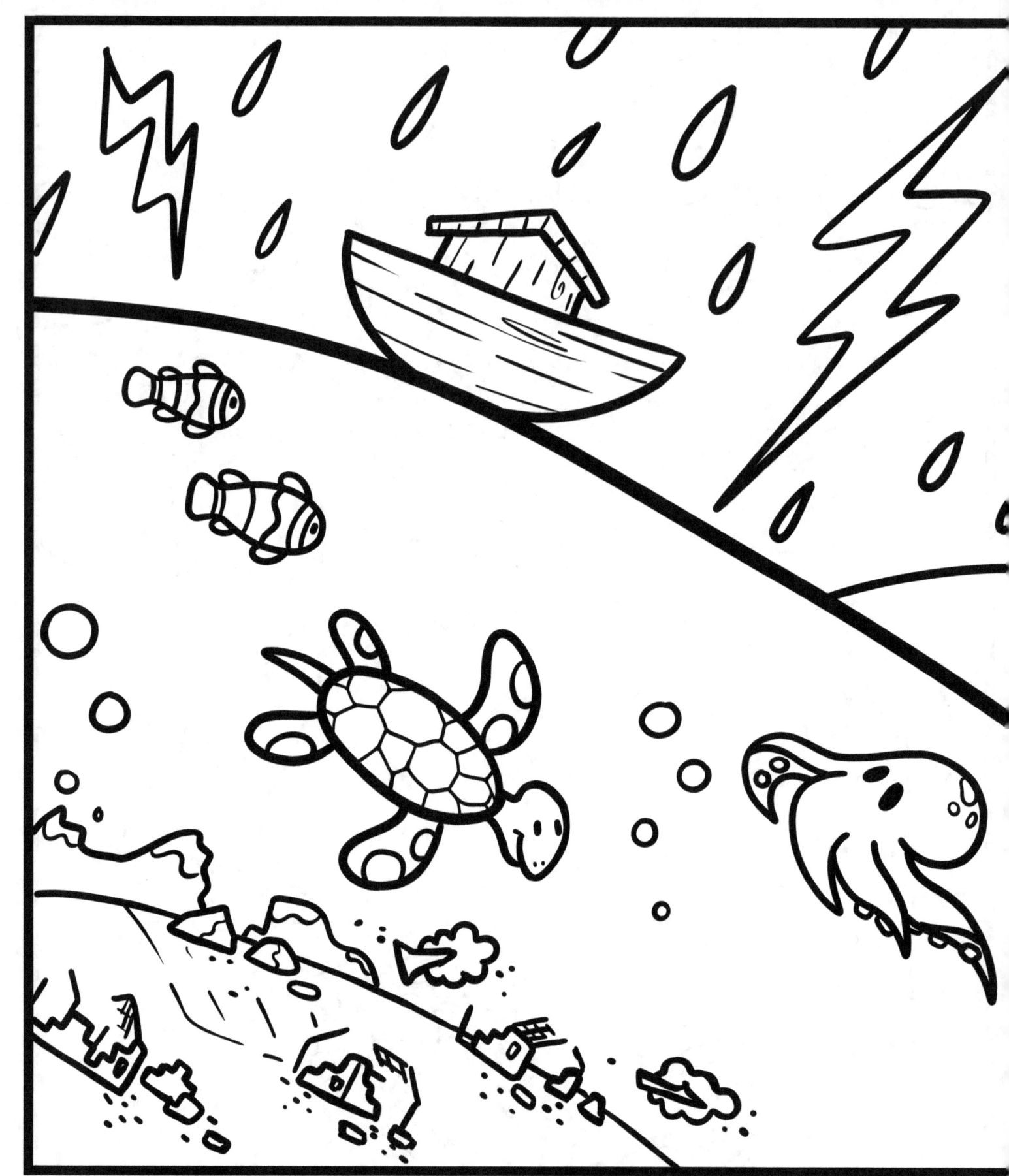

And the flood was forty days upon the earth;

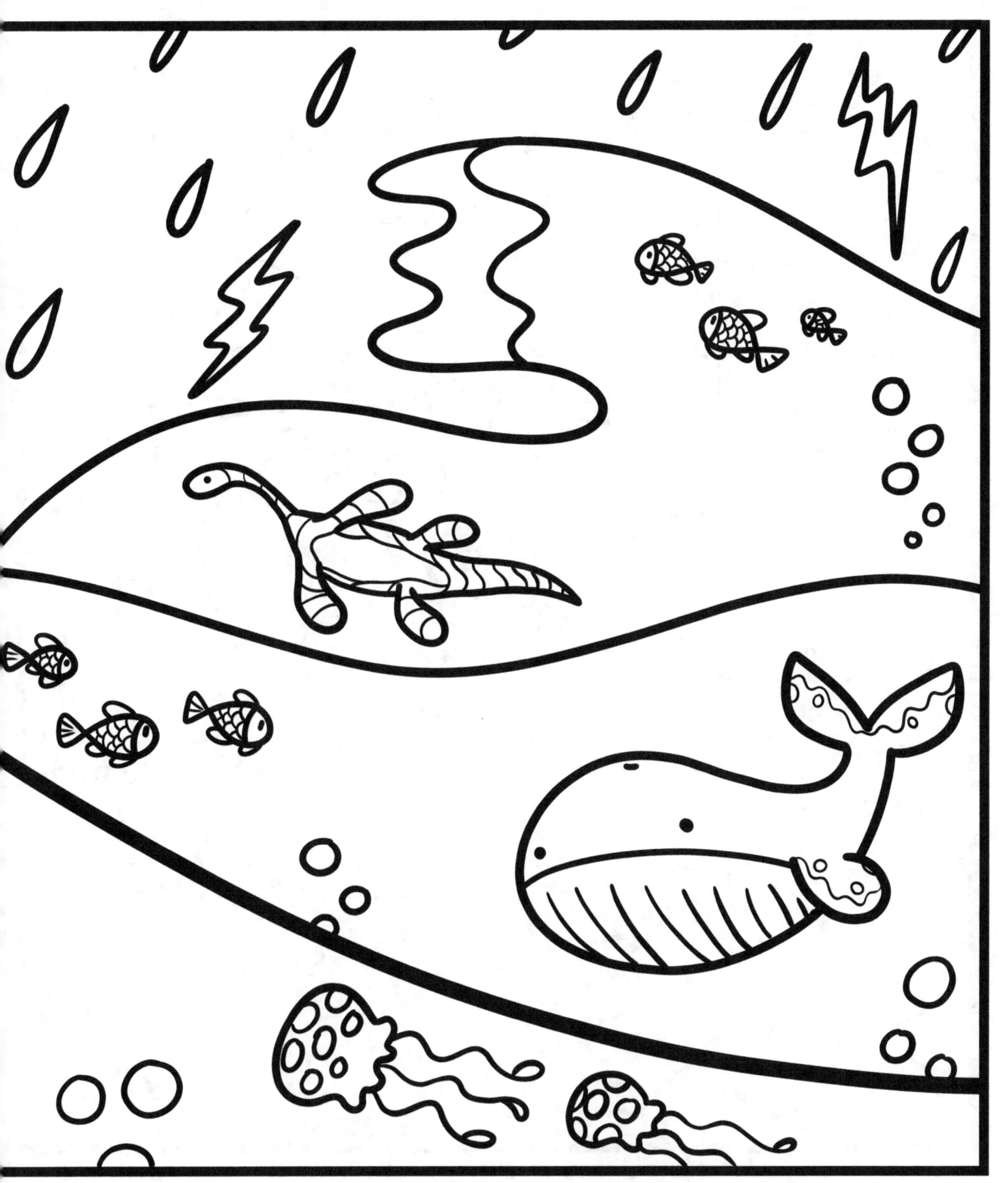

...and the waters increased, and bare up the ark, and it was lift up above the earth. Genesis 7:17

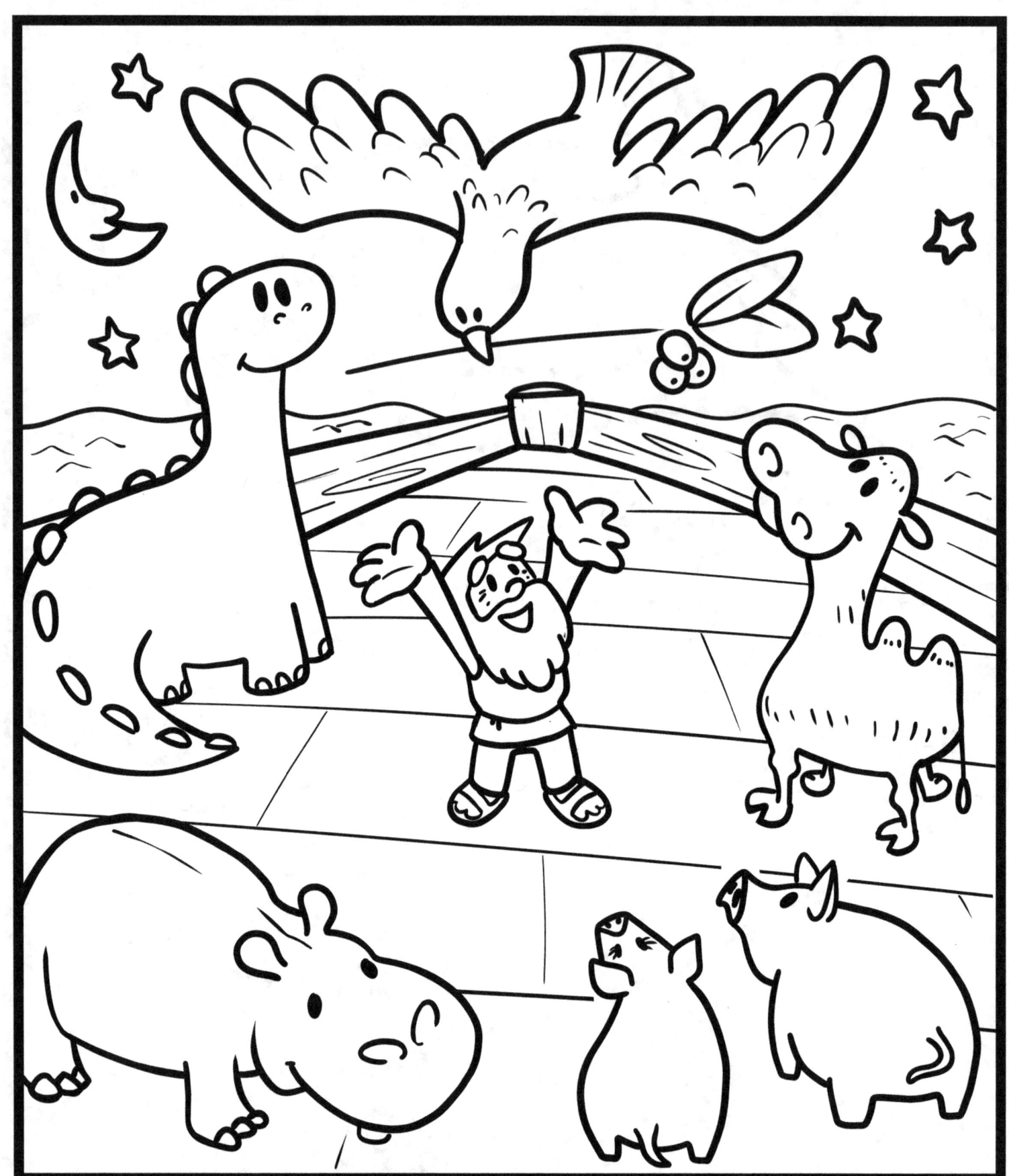

And he stayed yet other seven days; and again he sent forth the dove out of the ark; and the dove came in to him in the evening; and, lo, in her mouth was an olive leaf pluckt off: so Noah knew that the waters were abated from off the earth.

Genesis 8:10-11

And Noah builded an altar unto the Lord ; and took of every clean beast, and of every clean fowl, and offered burnt offerings on the altar. And the Lord smelled a sweet savour; and the Lord said in his heart, I will not again curse the ground any more for man's sake; for the imagination of man's heart is evil from his youth; neither will I again smite any more every thing living, as I have done.

Genesis 8:20-21

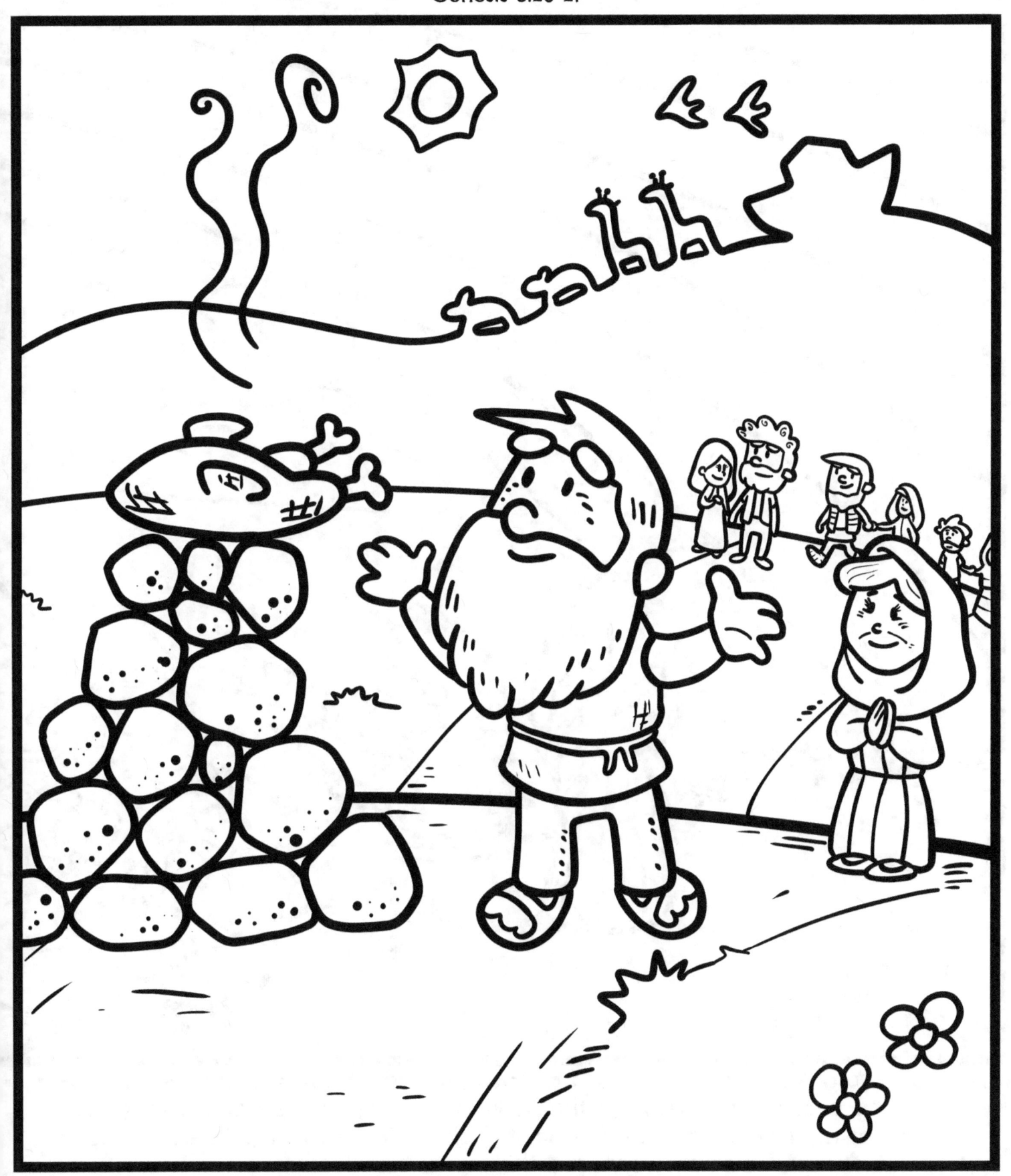

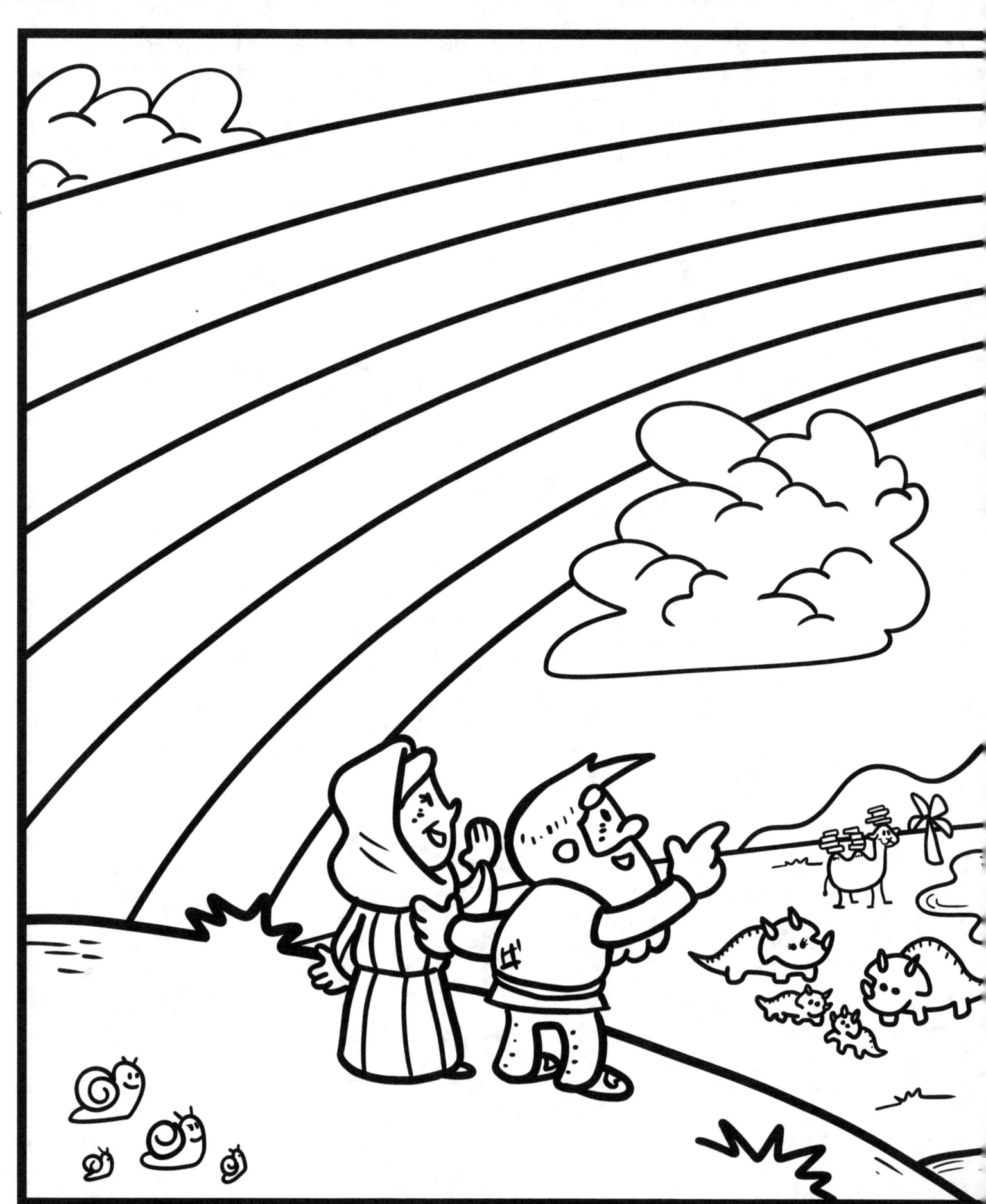

And God said, This is the token of the covenant which I make between me and
you and every living creature that is with you, for perpetual generations:
I do set my bow in the cloud, and it shall be for a token of a covenant
between me and the earth. Genesis 9:12-13

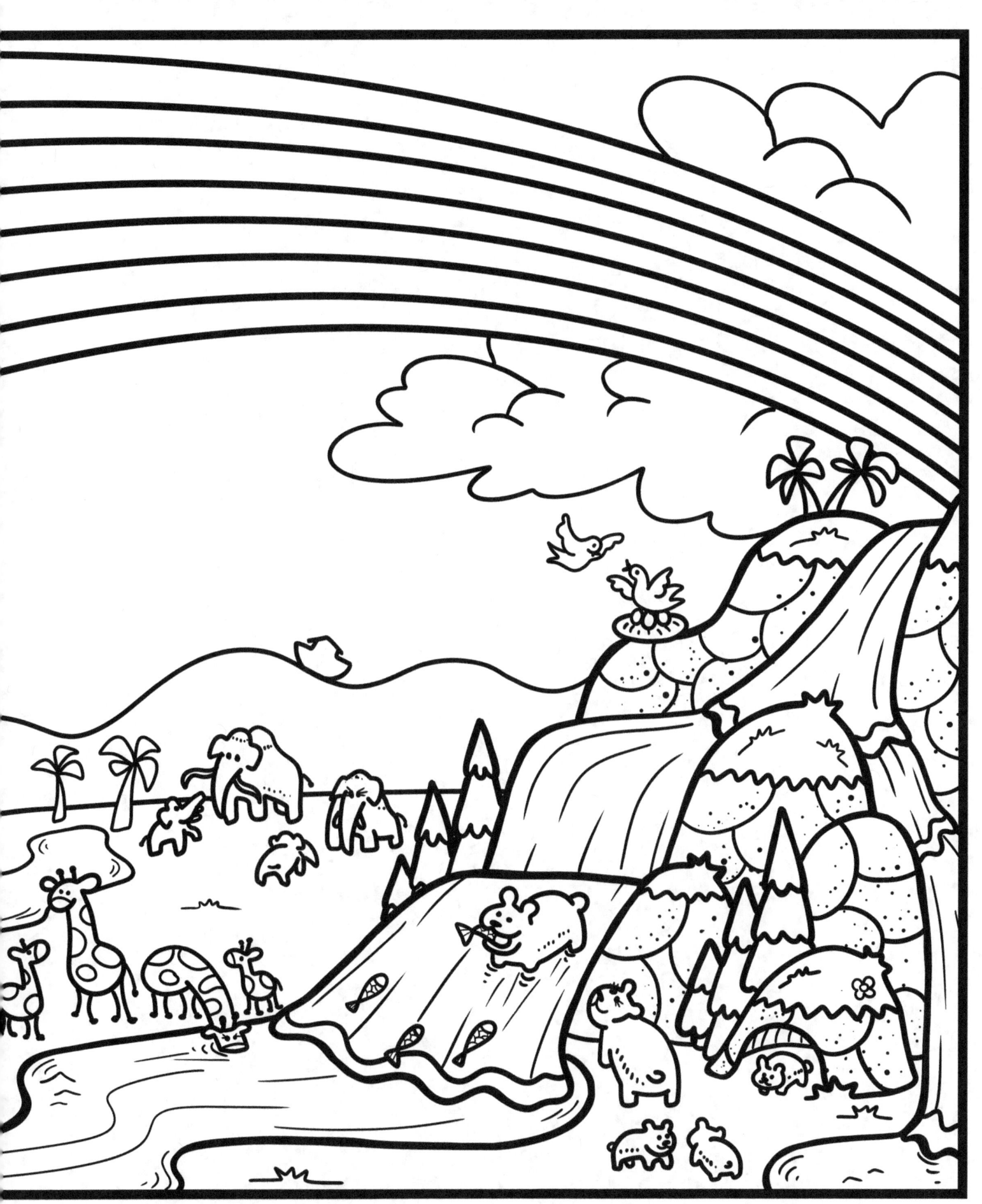

And I will remember my covenant, which is between me and you and every
living creature of all flesh; and the waters shall no more become
a flood to destroy all flesh. Genesis 9:15

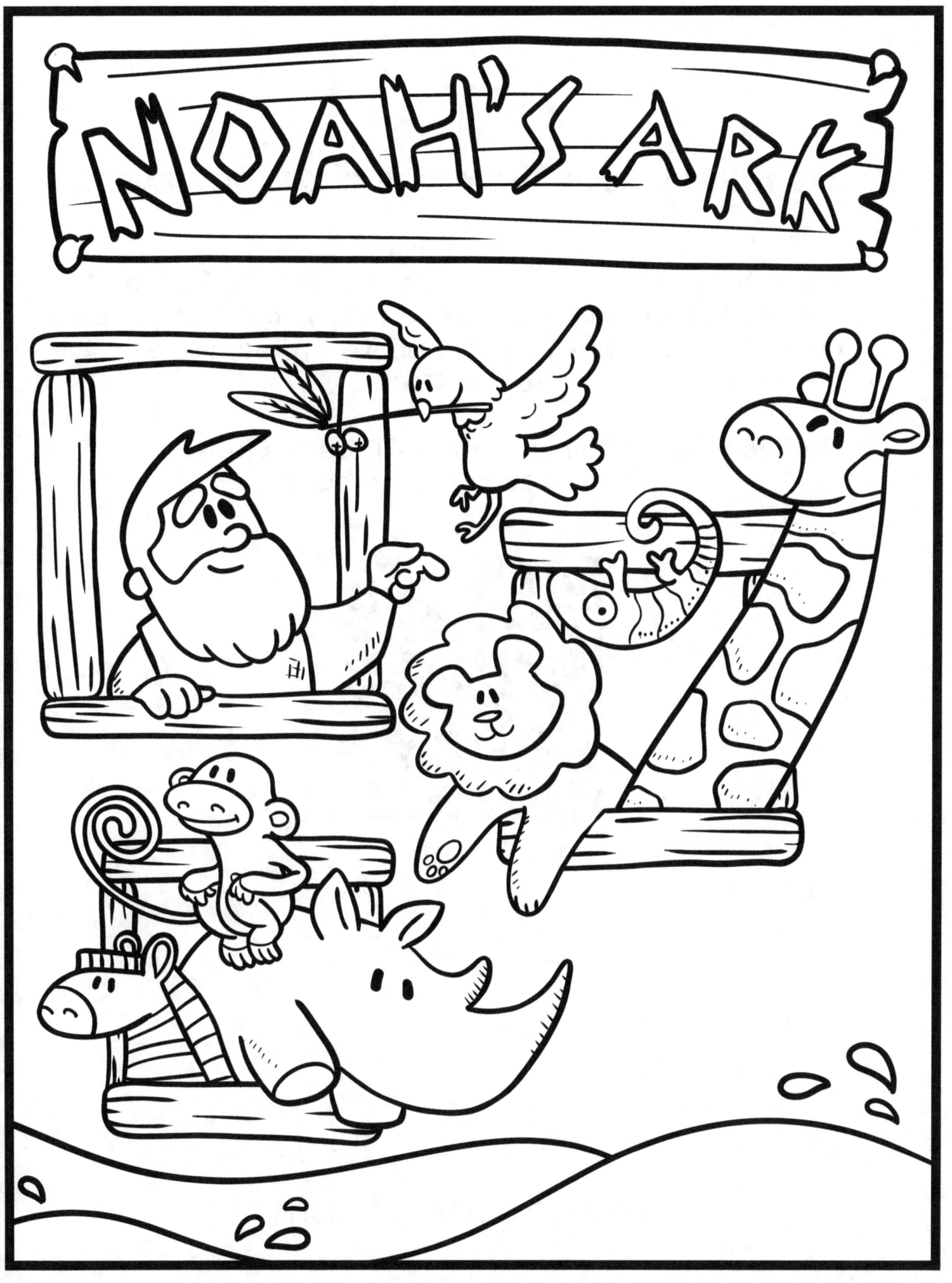

ARE YOU 100% SURE THAT YOU'RE GOING TO HEAVEN?

1 John 5:13
"These things have I written unto you that believe on the name of the Son of God; that ye may know that ye have eternal life, and that ye may believe on the name of the Son of God."

To know for certain, scan the QR code below or visit thebookcamel.com/heaven

theBookCamel.com